SCHOLASTIC

READ & RESPOND

Bringing the best books to life in the classroom

Activities based on The Twits

By Roald Dahl

CW00820014

Terms and conditions
IMPORTANT – PERMITTED USE AND WARNINGS – READ CAREFULLY BEFORE USING

This CD-ROM has been tested for viruses at all stages of its production. However, we recommend that you run virus-checking software on your computer systems at all times. Scholastic Ltd cannot accept any responsibility for any loss, disruption or damage to your data or your computer system that may occur as a result of using either the CD-ROM or the data held on it.

IF YOU ACCEPT THE ABOVE CONDITIONS YOU MAY PROCEED TO USE THE CD-ROM.

Recommended system requirements:
Windows: XP (Service Pack 3), Vista (Service Pack 2), Windows 7 or Windows 8 with 2.33GHz processor
Mac: OS 10.6 to 10.8 with Intel Core™ Duo processor
1GB RAM (recommended)
1024 x 768 Screen resolution
CD-ROM drive (24x speed recommended)
Adobe Reader (version 9 recommended for Mac users)
Broadband internet connections (for installation and updates)

For all technical support queries (including no CD drive), please phone Scholastic Customer Services on 0845 6039091.

Designed using Adobe Indesign
Published by Scholastic Ltd,
Book End, Range Road, Witney,
Oxfordshire OX29 0YD
www.scholastic.co.uk

Printed and bound by Ashford Colour Press
© 2015 Scholastic Ltd
1 2 3 4 5 6 7 8 9   5 6 7 8 9 0 1 2 3 4

British Library Cataloguing-in-Publication Data A catalogue record for this book is available from the British Library.
ISBN 978 1407 14222 7

Due to the nature of the web, we cannot guarantee the content or links of any site mentioned. We strongly recommend that teachers check websites before using them in the classroom.

Authors Debbie Ridgard and Sally Burt
Editorial team Rachel Morgan, Jenny Wilcox, Margaret Eaton, Red Door Media
Series designer Neil Salt
Design team Ian Foulis and Mike Connor
Illustrator Gemma Hastilow
Digital development Hannah Barnett, Phil Crothers and MWA Technologies Private Ltd

Acknowledgements
The publishers gratefully acknowledge permission to reproduce the following copyright material:
David Higham Associates for the use of text from *The Twits* by Roald Dahl, illustrated by Quentin Blake. Text © 1980, Roald Dahl Nominee Ltd (1980, Jonathan Cape Ltd). **A. P. Watt** for the electronic use of illustrations from *The Twits* by Roald Dahl, illustrated by Quentin Blake. Illustrations © 1980, Jonathan Cape Ltd). **Penguin Group UK** for the use of the cover from The Twits by Roald Dahl, illustrated by Quentin Blake. Text © 1980, Roald Dahl. Illustrations © 1980, Quentin Blake. (1980, Jonathan Cape Ltd).

Every effort has been made to trace copyright holders for the works reproduced in this book, and the publishers apologise for any inadvertent omissions.

CONTENTS

▼ INTRODUCTION

Read & Respond provides teaching ideas related to a specific children's book. The series focuses on best-loved books and brings you ways to use them to engage your class and enthuse them about reading.

The book is divided into different sections:

- **About the book and author:** gives you some background information about the book and the author.

- **Guided reading:** breaks the book down into sections and gives notes for using it with guided reading groups. A bookmark has been provided on page 8 containing comprehension questions. The children can be directed to refer to these as they read.

- **Shared reading:** provides extracts from the children's books with associated notes for focused work. There is also one non-fiction extract that relates to the children's book.

- **Grammar, punctuation & spelling:** provides word-level work related to the children's book so you can teach grammar, punctuation and spelling in context.

- **Plot, character & setting:** contains activity ideas focussed on the plot, characters and the setting of the story.

- **Talk about it:** has speaking and listening activities related to the children's book. These activities may be based directly on the children's book or be broadly based on the themes and concepts of the story.

- **Get writing:** provides writing activities related to the children's book. These activities may be based directly on the children's book or be broadly based on the themes and concepts of the story.

- **Assessment:** short activities that will help you assess whether the children have understood concepts and curriculum objectives. They are designed to be informal activities to feed into your planning.

The activities follow the same format:

- **Objective:** the objective for the lesson. It will be based upon a curriculum objective, but will often be more specific to the focus being covered.

- **What you need:** a list of resources you need to teach the lesson, including digital resources (printable pages, interactive activities and media resources, see page 5).

- **What to do:** the activity notes.

- **Differentiation:** this is provided where specific and useful differentiation advice can be given to support and/or extend the learning in the activity. Differentiation by providing additional adult support has not been included as this will be at a teacher's discretion based upon specific children's needs and ability, as well as the availability of support.

The activities are numbered for reference within each section and should move through the text sequentially– so you can use them while you are reading the book. Once you have read the book, most of the activities can be used in any order you wish.

elow are brief guidance notes for using the D-ROM. For more detailed information, please ick on the '?' button in the top right-hand corner f the screen.

he program contains the following:
- The extract pages from the book.
- All of the photocopiable pages from the book.
- Additional printable pages.
- Interactive on-screen activities.
- Media resources.

Getting started

ut the CD-ROM into your CD-ROM drive. If you o not have a CD-ROM drive, phone Scholastic ustomer Services on 0845 6039091.

For Windows users, the install wizard should autorun, if it fails to do so then navigate to your CD-ROM drive. Then follow the installation process.

For Mac users, copy the disk image file to your hard drive. After it has finished copying double click it to mount the disk image. Navigate to the mounted disk image and run the installer. After installation the disk image can be unmounted and the DMG can be deleted from the hard drive. To install on a network, please see the ReadMe file located on the CD-ROM (navigate to your drive).

complete the installation of the program you eed to open the program and click 'Update' in e pop-up. Please note – this CD-ROM is eb-enabled and the content will be downloaded om the internet to your hard-drive to populate e CD-ROM with the relevant resources. This only eeds to be done on first use, after this you will e able to use the CD-ROM without an internet nnection. If at any point any content is updated, u will receive another pop-up upon start up when ere is an internet connection.

Main menu

he main menu is the first screen that appears. Here u can access: terms and conditions, registration ks, how to use the CD-ROM and credits. To access specific book click on the relevant button (NB only les installed will be available). You can filter by the

drop-down lists if you wish. You can search all resources by clicking 'Search' in the bottom left-hand corner. You can also login and access favourites that you have bookmarked.

Resources

By clicking on a book on the main menu, you are taken to the resources for that title. The resources are: Media, Interactives, Extracts and Printables. Select the category and then launch a resource by clicking the play button.

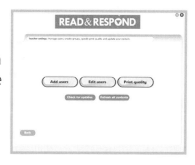

Teacher settings

In the top right-hand corner of the screen is a small 'T' icon. This is the teacher settings area. It is password protected, the password is: login. This area will allow you to choose the print quality settings for interactive activities ('Default' or 'Best') and also allow you to check for updates to the program or re-download all content to the disk via Refresh all content. It is from here that you can set up user logins so that you can save and access favourites. Once a user is set up, they can enter by clicking the login link underneath the 'T' and '?' buttons.

Search

You can access an all resources search by clicking the search button on the bottom-left of the main menu. You can search for activities by type (using the drop-down filter) or by keyword by typing into the box. You can then assign resources to your favourites area or launch them directly from the search area.

CURRICULUM LINKS

Section	Activity	Curriculum objectives
Guided reading		Comprehension: To develop positive attitudes to reading and understanding of what they read.
Shared reading	1	Comprehension: To discuss words and phrases that capture the reader's interest and imagination.
	2	Comprehension: To read aloud and show understanding through intonation, tone, volume and action.
	3	Comprehension: To draw inferences such as inferring characters' feelings, thoughts and motives from their actions.
	4	Comprehension: To identify main ideas and summarise these.
Grammar, punctuation & spelling	1	Word reading: To apply their growing knowledge of root words, prefixes and suffixes and to understand the meaning of new words that they meet.
	2	Transcription: To use suffixes and understand how to add them.
	3	Composition: To use and punctuate direct speech.
	4	Transcription: To place the possessive apostrophe accurately in words with regular plurals.
	5	Composition: To use fronted adverbials.
	6	Word reading: To show how words are related in form and meaning.
Plot, character & setting	1	Composition: To create characters.
	2	Composition: To use simple organisational devices.
	3	Composition: To discuss writing similar to that which they are planning to write in order to understand and learn from its structure, vocabulary and grammar.
	4	Composition: To identify main ideas and summarise these.
	5	Composition: To create settings, characters and plot.
	6	Composition: To understand what they read by asking questions to improve their understanding of a text.
	7	Spoken language: To participate in role play.
	8	Composition: To progressively build a varied and rich vocabulary and an increasing range of sentence structures.

Section	Activity	Curriculum objectives
Talk about it	1	Spoken language: To participate in presentations.
	2	Spoken language: To participate in role play.
	3	Spoken language: To participate in discussions.
	4	Spoken language: To use spoken language to develop understanding through imagining and exploring ideas.
	5	Spoken language: To speak audibly and fluently with an increasing command of standard English.
	6	Spoken language: To articulate and justify answers, arguments and opinions.
Get writing	1	Composition: To use simple organisational devices.
	2	Composition: To retrieve and record information from non-fiction.
	3	Composition: To discuss writing similar to that which they are planning to write in order to understand and learn from its structure, vocabulary and grammar.
	4	Composition: To plan their writing by discussing and recording ideas.
	5	Composition: To use simple organisational devices.
	6	Composition: To read aloud their own writing using appropriate intonation and controlling the tone and volume.
Assessment	1	Comprehension: To check that the text makes sense to them, discussing their understanding and explaining the meaning of words in context.
	2	Comprehension: To understand what they read by asking questions to improve their understanding of a text.
	3	Spoken language: To speak audibly and fluently with an increasing command of standard English.
	4	Comprehension: To draw inferences such as inferring characters' feelings, thoughts and motives from their actions, and justifying inferences with evidence.
	5	Composition: To proofread for spelling and punctuation errors.
	6	Comprehension: To identify themes and conventions in a wide range of books.

▼ THE TWITS

About the book

One of Roald Dahl's timeless stories for young readers but enjoyed by all ages, *The Twits* introduces Mr and Mrs Twit, probably the most awful couple you'll ever meet! Not only do they look awful, but they also enjoy doing cruel, horrible things to each other and to others.

Mr Twit has a thick, dirty beard that he never washes. Stuck to it are bits of revolting leftovers, which he snacks on when peckish. Mrs Twit is a good match for Mr Twit. She is just as smelly, ugly and mean as her husband. The couple live in a windowless house and spend their time cooking up evil plans to trick each other. To make his favourite dish, bird pie, Mr Twit ensnares unfortunate birds by smearing glue on the branches of the dead tree outside the house! They own a family of mistreated, former circus monkeys that are made to stand on their heads all day so Mr Twit can use them in his 'upside-down circus'. Just when there seems no end to the Twits' cruelty, the monkeys, together with the clever Roly-Poly Bird from Africa, come up with an ingenious plan. This ultimate monkey trick gives these two horrible people exactly what they deserve!

The story is told in the familiar Roald Dahl style that readers everywhere enjoy: wicked humour, evil villains and twists in the tale, making it a favourite among younger readers. One of Dahl's best known quotes is found in this story in the description of Mrs Twit: 'A person who has good thoughts cannot ever be ugly.'

About the author

Roald Dahl was born in Wales in 1916 to Norwegian parents but grew up in England. As a child, Dahl was an avid reader but he didn't do well at school. His family suffered tragedy when his older sister and father died within weeks of each other when he was only three years old. His eventful childhood is perhaps the source of the many colourful and creative ideas that appear in his hugely popular stories.

After establishing himself as an adult story writer, Dahl began writing stories for children in 1960. His first stories were written for his own five children, whom he believed enjoyed being frightened as well as disgusted! He understood the magic of drawing in his readers with larger-than-life characters, twisted plots and good triumphing over evil.

About the illustrator

Roald Dahl teamed up successfully for many of his books with illustrator Sir Quentin Blake who is himself a popular cartoonist and writer. Blake's humorous illustrations perfectly complement Roald Dahl's mischievous and witty style.

Key Facts

The Twits

Author: Roald Dahl

Illustration: Quentin Blake

First published: 1980 by Jonathan Cape Ltd

Awards: Roald Dahl won the World Fantasy Convention Lifetime Achievement Award in 1983.

Did you know: Roald Dahl wrote his books in a brick hut which was on the edge of the orchard at Gypsy house.

A hairy beginning

Together with the class, look at the cover of the book. Ask: *What is a twit? Do you know other similar words?* (Idiot, silly person, nitwit, moron, twerp.) *Are they nice or nasty words? Are the words formal or informal?* ('Twit', 'idiot' and 'silly' can be used formally but the others are informal.) Ask the children why 'Twits' is spelled with a capital letter. (It is a proper noun in this context.)

Refer to question 6 on the Guided Reading bookmark (page 12). Ask: *What clues do the illustrations provide about the Twits?* (Covers vary but many show Mr and Mrs Twit standing on their heads, foreshadowing what is to come.) *From the illustrations, what sort of people do they seem to be? Can you judge from how they look?* Discuss expressions such as 'never judge a book by its cover' and 'never judge a man by his overcoat'. Ask: *How are these expressions similar?* (Both remind us not to judge a person's character based on appearance.)

Next, read the blurb on the back cover and ask what more we learn about the characters and story. (Mean, unhappy characters; possible theme of revenge; humorous genre.)

Ask who has read other Roald Dahl books. What do the children expect from a Roald Dahl story? (Humour, revenge, larger-than-life characters, good triumphing over evil, twisted plots.)

Read the first chapter together. Ask: *Who is the narrator talking to?* (The reader.) *What does the narrator want to know?* (How often do bearded men wash their faces?) *Is it an unusual story beginning? Why? Is it serious or funny?* (Unusual and funny – it gets readers' attention.) *What does it tell us about the author's likes and dislikes?* (Apparently Roald Dahl hated beards.) *What is it called when you dislike someone simply because of appearance?* (Prejudice.) *What is it called when you generalise about people's characteristics?* (Stereotyping – for example, believing that all people with beards are wise.) Show the children images of people with beards (such as Father Christmas, Rasputin, Socrates, King Henry VIII, Abraham Lincoln) and discuss their opinions.

Meet the Twits

Read chapters 2, 3 and 4 aloud to the children. They should formulate a mind picture of the characters before viewing the illustrations in the book.

Together, look at the illustrations. Ask: *How do the illustrations match the character descriptions?* (Cartoon-type pictures exaggerate features and stress the absurdity and humour in the text.)

Read the text again with the children following. Ask: *In what ways are Mr and Mrs Twit similar?* (Both are ugly, dirty, rude and cruel.) *What is unique to each character?* (Mr Twit's dirty beard; Mrs Twit's glass eye and walking stick.)

Discuss the deeper meaning behind why Mr and Mrs Twit are so ugly. Ask: *Is Mr Twit ugly because of his beard?* (No, his beard is dirty and he doesn't wash.) *Is Mrs Twit ugly because of her glass eye?* (No, bad thoughts make her ugly.) *Can you tell by their descriptions whether the main characters are 'good' or 'bad'?*

What goes around…

Together with the class, read chapters 5 to 8 ('The Glass Eye' to 'The Funny Walking Stick'). Ask: *What do the Twits do to each other? Why?* (They play awful tricks on each other for revenge – each trick is paid back with a worse one!) *What do you think happens next?* Talk about different types of practical jokes that the children might know (jack-in-the-box, whoopee cushion and so on). Discuss how each trick in the book works, and talk about a possible trick that might happen next.

Now continue reading to the end of the chapter 'Mrs Twit Goes Ballooning Up'. Ask: *Do you feel sorry for Mrs Twit? What would you do if you were her?* Give your own ideas to start off the discussion. Then read the next few chapters to find out how she really reacts!

Ask the children to identify the story pattern so far. (The characters are intent on paying back one nasty trick for another.) From this, can the children identify the main theme of the plot line? (Revenge.) Ask them to discuss question 14 on the bookmark (see page 12).

Next, read together to the end of the chapter 'Four Sticky Little Boys'. Ask: *How did Mr Twit trick the birds? Do the Twits treat others any differently to how they treat each other? What evidence is there? What do you think Mr Twit would have done with the boys if he had caught them?*

The plot thickens

Continue reading to the end of chapter 21, 'Mr and Mrs Twit Go Off to Buy Guns'. Ask: *What other characters have been introduced?* (The birds, the monkeys, the Roly-Poly Bird from Africa.) *Can you give evidence to show how the Twits treat them?* (They are all mistreated – for example, the birds are glued to the tree, and the monkeys are kept in a small cage and made to do everything upside down.)

Ask: *What is a Roly-Poly Bird?* (An imaginary bird.) Show the children a large map of the world. Discuss the route and distances the Roly-Poly Bird might have taken to reach England from Africa.

With the class, read the title of the next chapter, 'Muggle-Wump Has an Idea'. Ask: *What idea do you think he has?* Before reading ahead, predict how the animals might get their revenge. Ask: *Is this the turning point or climax? How can you tell?* (Different characters take centre stage and the animals' fortunes start to change as they gain the upper hand.)

A sticky end

Read the rest of the book's chapter headings – they provide a summary of the ending. Ask: *From the chapter headings, can you predict how the* story ends? Discuss various ideas.

After discussing the chapter titles, read together to the end of the book. Talk about how the animals got their revenge by playing a nasty trick on the Twits. Ask: *Did the Twits get what they deserved? Is it right to hope they did?*

Second reading

Use subsequent readings to explore key features of the novel in more depth. Use questions on the Guided Reading Bookmark (page 12) to help focus discussions.

Structure

Divide the book into sections to reflect the plot structure:

- Chapters 1–13: Describe the characters and the awful tricks they play on each other.
- Chapters 14–21: Introduce the other characters and describe the problem that the Twits face.
- Chapters 22–27: Describe how the story's 'victims' take revenge by playing an awful trick.
- Chapters 28–29: Conclude the story and discuss what happens to all the characters.

Note how the middle chapters (14 and 15) change from one topic to another; the focus shifts to the story's other characters, which sets the scene for the next part of the story. Encourage the children to think about how the story structure conveys the message 'what goes around comes around'. The tricks described at the beginning are what lead to the Twits' sticky end! Can the children think of similar expressions?

Style

As you read through the book with the class, draw attention to Quentin Blake's illustrations. Ask: *How do the drawings complement the story? Were*

...ey planned to be part of the story? Point out that ...e narrator sometimes refers to the pictures – for ...ample, in the chapter entitled 'Mrs Twit' the text ...ys 'Take a look at her' and in the chapter 'The ...ouse, the Tree and the Monkey Cage' it says 'Here ...a picture of Mr and Mrs Twit's house and garden.'

Point out how the narrator uses second-person ...arrative, appearing to speak to the reader as if ...ader and narrator are having a conversation, ...aring the same view.

Note how Roald Dahl uses expressive dialogue ...mong the characters to tell most of the story, ...nd how he uses punctuation and capitalisation ...r effect.

Humour is important in the story along with ...xaggerated characters and absurd plot. Dahl ...ombines the real and the imaginary to create ...n intriguing tale.

...etting

...ncourage the children to think about how the ...wits' home and its surroundings contribute to the ...haracterisation and atmosphere. The house with ...o windows is dark and unwelcoming – just like the ...wners. The tree outside the house is dead; the only ...lants are thorns and thistles. The setting reflects ...he cruel, mean nature of the Twits and adds to the ...evulsion and aversion felt by the other characters ...nd the reader. Ask: *How does the description of ...he setting add to the humour and ridiculousness ...f the story?* (The idea of a house with no windows ...nd a dead garden is bizarre. The author has ...xaggerated the features of the setting, as with ...he characters.)

Themes

When they have finished re-reading the text, ask the children to reflect on the key themes: revenge, good triumphing over evil, what goes around comes around, team work, kindness, respect, hygiene and first impressions. Refer to the interactive activity 'Exploring themes' to help guide this discussion.

Discuss question 11 on page 12. Think of common expressions and idioms that describe the book's themes, such as 'an eye for an eye', 'what goes around, comes around', 'what goes up, must come down', 'many hands make light work' and 'two wrongs don't make a right'. Match them to events in the story.

■SCHOLASTIC
READ&RESPOND
Bringing the best books to life in the classroom

The Twits
by Roald Dahl

Focus on...
Meaning

1. Explain the significance of the characters' names.

2. Predict what happens in the story from each chapter title.

3. Is 'the shrinks' a real disease? How do you know?

4. What other lies are told in the story?

Focus on...
Organisation

5. What is the effect of having many, short chapters?

6. How do the illustrations complement the book?

7. What devices does the author use to engage the reader?

8. If you divide the book into two parts, what is the focus of each half?

■SCHOLASTIC
READ&RESPOND
Bringing the best books to life in the classroom

The Twits
by Roald Dahl

Focus on...
Language and features

9. Which 'twit' synonyms best fit the Twits? What other words could you choose?

10. How do the pictures help tell the story?

11. Which common sayings describe the events and themes in the story?

12. Identify the made-up words and names. Do they mean anything?

Focus on...
Purpose, viewpoints and effects

13. Which characters would you like/not like to meet? Why?

14. Which trick was the worst? Why?

15. Does the author suggest that playing tricks is a good or bad thing? What do you think?

16. According to the author, what makes a person ugly? Do you agree?

17. Who are the heroes in the story? Can heroes also do bad things?

Extract 1

- Read together an enlarged copy of Extract 1. Ask: *Is Mrs Twit similar to or different from her husband? Which sentence tells us this?* (Similar: 'Mrs Twit was no better than her husband.' Different: 'Mrs Twit wasn't born ugly.')

- Get the children to underline words and phrases describing Mrs Twit. Ask: *Which word is repeated for effect?* ('Ugly'.) *How many forms of this word can you find?* ('Ugly' – adjective, 'uglier' – comparative adjective, 'ugliness' – abstract noun.) *What is the effect of the repetition?* (It emphasises the word.)

- Ask the children to circle adjectives that describe Mrs Twit's facial features. (Wonky nose, stick-out teeth.) *What other words could the author have used?*

- Locate the word 'nice' in Extract 1. What does it describe? (Mrs Twit's face when younger.) Can the children suggest some appropriate synonyms that can be used to replace 'nice' in this context? (Lovely, pretty, sweet, attractive.)

- Now locate the simile: '…they will shine out of your face like sunbeams.' Ask: *What is being compared to what?* (Good thoughts are compared to sunbeams.) Discuss other similes in the book such as Mr Twit's hair 'It grew in spikes like the bristles of a nailbrush' and 'She went up like a rocket.'

- Consider the style. Ask: *Is it formal or friendly? Is it fact or opinion? What does it mean to have an opinion?* (One person's point of view; not necessarily shared by everyone.)

- The author uses different narrative forms to convey his point of view and describe Mrs Twit. Point out examples of third person narrative (She did not...have a hairy face…); first person (I doubt it, I'll tell you why…); and second person (if you have good thoughts…) Ask: *What effect does this have?* (It seems like the narrator is speaking directly to the reader.)

Extract 2

- Choose three volunteers (two characters and a narrator) to read Extract 2 aloud with expression.

- Point out the exclamation marks. Ask: *What effect do they have?* (They highlight emotions of fear, surprise and panic expressed in the text.)

- Circle each occurrence of 'SHRINK/S'. Ask: *Why has the author used capital letters?* (For emphasis – Mr Twit is scaring Mrs Twit by repeating the word.) *How does the repetition affect the pace of the text?* (It slows it down. You can almost hear Mr Twit speaking slowly and clearly.)

- Consider sentence length. Ask the children to underline Mrs Twit's sentences. What do they notice about their length? (They are all short.) How does this affect the tone and pace of what she says? (They speed up the pace and show her growing panic.)

- Highlight the inverted commas indicating direct speech. Ask: *How does direct speech help tell this part of the story?* (The dialogue is entertaining and gives the reader insight into what the characters feel and think.) Do the children think that this part would be as enjoyable if told in reported speech, such as: 'Then he told her that… and she gasped and pleaded with him?' (No, the effect would be lost.)

- Circle the verbs 'said' and 'cried'. Ask: *What other verbs could be used instead?*

- Read the last line. Ask: *Why is the word 'stretched' in italics?* (For emphasis.)

Extract 3

- Together, read an enlarged copy of Extract 3. Ask: *What tense is it written in?* (Past.)

- Consider dialogue use. Ask: *Has the author used any dialogue to tell this part of the story?* (No.) *What effect does this have?* (It feels like the narrator is breaking away from the characters to give the reader insights into the setting and their other activities.) *Is first or second person narrative used in this part?* (No.) *What is this chapter's purpose?* (It sets the scene for the next part of the story.)

- Circle the capitalised words. What is their purpose? (Capitalised words create effect or highlight names: *The Big Dead Tree, Bird Pie day, HUGTIGHT glue*.)

- Ask: *Which day is Bird Pie day?* (Wednesday.) Can the children invent a name for the day before? (For example, Bird-catch day, Glue day.)

- Locate the statement, 'Mr Twit was good at catching birds.' Is it serious, bitter, funny, sarcastic or silly? (It sounds serious but when you read how he catches birds you realise it is sarcastic. He wasn't 'good' at catching birds; he was 'good' at tricking them.)

- Encourage the children to think of adjectives and phrases to describe the Twits. Extract 3 does not directly describe the Twits but what does it reveal about them? (It reveals their awful behaviour from which the reader can infer what they are like.)

Extract 4

- Highlight the title of Extract 4, 'Who invented glue?'. Discuss possible answers, allowing the children to give opinions and ideas. Find out their prior knowledge. Ask: *Do you think glue is an important part of our lives? How many uses for glue can you think of? Apart from glue, how else can you stick things together?* (Putty, Velcro, sticky tape and so on.) *How did people manage before glue?* (Most cultures came up with their own ways – for example, Japanese people used sticky rice as cement.)

- Now read the rest of Extract 4 together. Discuss the genre and style of writing and compare it to the previous extracts. Ask: *Is this text fiction or non-fiction? Descriptive or informative? Does it have facts, opinions or both?* Identify unfamiliar words and discuss their meanings in context.

- Use the internet or an encyclopedia to find a good close-up photograph of a gecko. Draw the children's attention to its specialised feet that enable it to stick to smooth surfaces, even when walking upside down on a ceiling.

- Consider the text organisation. Number the paragraphs. Ask: *Would it make a difference if the text was all in one paragraph?* (The heading and short paragraphs make it clearer and more readable.) Identify the main idea of each section and label them on the page (1 – title, 2 – natural glues, 3 – synthetic glues, 4 – animal glues).

- Underline the key words in the text. These should be the main verbs, nouns and important adjectives. The word 'glue' does not have to be underlined as it is implied.

- Draw a mind map using key words to show the main ideas in each section of the text.

Extract 1

Mrs Twit

Mrs Twit was no better than her husband.

She did not, of course, have a hairy face. It was a pity she didn't because that at any rate would have hidden some of her fearful ugliness.

Take a look at her.

Have you ever seen a woman with an uglier face than that? I doubt it.

But the funny thing is that Mrs Twit wasn't born ugly. She'd had quite a nice face when she was young. The ugliness had grown upon her year by year as she got older.

Why would that happen? I'll tell you why.

If a person has ugly thoughts, it begins to show on the face. And when that person has ugly thoughts every day, every week, every year, the face gets uglier and uglier until it gets so ugly you can hardly bear to look at it.

A person who has good thoughts cannot ever be ugly. You can have a wonky nose and a crooked mouth and a double chin and stick-out teeth, but if you have good thoughts they will shine out of your face like sunbeams and you will always look lovely.

Nothing good shone out of Mrs Twit's face.
In her right hand she carried a walking-stick. She used to tell people that this was because she had warts growing on the sole of her left foot and walking was painful. But the real reason she carried a stick was so that she could hit things with it, things like dogs and cats and small children.

And then there was the glass eye. Mrs Twit had a glass eye that was always looking the other way.

Extract 2

Mrs Twit Has the Shrinks

'You've got the *shrinks*!' cried Mr Twit, pointing his finger at her like a pistol. 'You've got them badly! You've got the most terrible case of shrinks I've ever seen!'

Mrs Twit became so frightened she began to dribble. But Mr Twit, still remembering the worms in his spaghetti, didn't feel sorry for her at all. 'I suppose you know what *happens* to you when you get the shrinks?' he said.

'What?' gasped Mrs Twit. 'What happens?'

'Your head SHRINKS into your neck…

'And your neck SHRINKS into your body…

'And your body SHRINKS into your legs…

'And your legs SHRINK into your feet. And in the end there's nothing left except a pair of shoes and a bundle of old clothes.'

'I can't bear it!' cried Mrs Twit.

'It's a terrible disease,' said Mr Twit. 'The worst in the world.'

'How long have I got?' cried Mrs Twit. 'How long before I finish up as a bundle of old clothes and a pair of shoes?'

"Mr Twit put on a very solemn face. 'At the rate you're going,' he said, shaking his head sadly, 'I'd say not more than ten or eleven days.'

'But isn't there *anything* we can do?' cried Mrs Twit.

There's only one cure for the shrinks,' said Mr Twit.

'Tell me!' she cried. 'Oh, tell me quickly!'

'We'll have to hurry!' said Mr Twit.

'I'm ready. I'll hurry! I'll do anything you say!' cried Mrs Twit.

'You won't last long if you don't,' said Mr Twit, giving her another grizzly grin.

'What is it I must do?' cried Mrs Twit, clutching her cheeks.

'You've got to be *stretched*,' said Mr Twit.

Extract 3

Hugtight Sticky Glue

Once a week, on Wednesdays, the Twits had Bird Pie for supper. Mr Twit caught the birds and Mrs Twit cooked them.

Mr Twit was good at catching birds. On the day before Bird Pie day, he would put the ladder up against The Big Dead Tree and climb into the branches with a bucket of glue and a paint-brush. The glue he used was something called HUGTIGHT and it was stickier than any other glue in the world. He would paint it along the tops of all the branches and then go away.

As the sun went down, birds would fly in from all around to roost for the night in The Big Dead Tree. They didn't know, poor things, that the branches were all smeared with horrible HUGTIGHT. The moment they landed on a branch, their feet stuck and that was that.

The next morning, which was Bird Pie day, Mr Twit would climb up the ladder again and grab all the wretched birds that were stuck to the tree. It didn't matter what kind they were – song thrushes, blackbirds, sparrows, crows, little jenny wrens, robins, anything – they all went into the pot for Wednesday's Bird Pie supper.

Extract 4

Who invented glue?

It's difficult to say exactly who invented glue. The earliest evidence of glue is found in ancient cave paintings. The artists mixed glue with natural pigments (like berry juice or clay) to make the paint stick to the walls. The glue was different then. It was made from plant and animal extracts like tree sap, plant gum, animal bones, hooves, fat or blood, beeswax, egg white or corn starch. These early inventors would mix, boil and mash natural ingredients into a sticky paste for fixing and building.

It was only in the early 20th century that synthetic (man-made) adhesives (sticky substances) were invented. They stuck better and were cheaper and easier to produce. In 1942, an inventor by the name of Dr Harry Coover stumbled upon a super sticky substance. It was sticking to everything and was a real nuisance until he realised it was something quite extraordinary. He named it 'Superglue'. 'Superglue' is so super, that a patch the size of a matchbox can hold up a small car!

While humans have been discovering and inventing glue, nature has its own glue technology that holds the key to how things really stick! Barnacles use a type of natural cement to attach themselves to boats, rocks and even whales. Then there's slug slime. Snails and slugs store dry mucus granules that turn to goo when they're excreted – just like glue powder! But the most amazing of all is the gecko – a little lizard that can walk up windows or crawl along a ceiling with its sticky feet! Millions of tiny sticky hairs on its toe pads allow the feet to attach or detach to any surface with no mess. Based on these amazing sticky feet, scientists have invented a new super-adhesive called Geckskin™ that can hold a TV or computer safely onto a wall without leaving marks!

Did you know?
The first glue factory was founded in Holland in 1690 where glue was made from natural products.

GRAMMAR, PUNCTUATION & SPELLING

1. Prefixes have purpose

Objective

To use prefixes to change words so they have opposite meanings.

What you need

Copies of *The Twits*, photocopiable page 22 'Picky prefixes', interactive activity 'Growing roots'.

What to do

- Together with the class, read chapters 1–4 in the book. Ask the children to think of word pairs with opposite meanings, such as clean/dirty, and ugly/beautiful. Show them that some words can change to the opposite meaning by adding a prefix (for example, clean/unclean).

- Revise root words. Remind the children that a root word (or base word) is the form of the word that cannot be made smaller. Prefixes (or suffixes) are added to root words to change their meaning or purpose. The interactive activity 'Growing roots' can be used to reinforce this concept.

- In chapters 1–4, negative words are used to describe Mr and Mrs Twit as nasty people. Ask the children to complete photocopiable page 22 'Picky prefixes', changing the words into negative words by adding the appropriate prefixes: kind (unkind), loving (unloving), tasteful (distasteful), agreeable (disagreeable), satisfied (dissatisfied), patient (impatient), willing (unwilling), happy (unhappy), social (antisocial), obedient (disobedient), polite (impolite).

- Ask the children to use some of these words to write a short paragraph describing Mr and Mrs Twit.

Differentiation

Support: Provide other examples for children to identify the root word by removing the prefix and/or suffix.

Extension: Encourage children to use dictionaries to find other words with prefixes that change the word to have an opposite meaning. They can also research other prefixes and their functions ('re', 'sub', 'inter', 'auto' and so on).

2. Sly suffixes

Objective

To add the suffix 'ly' onto adjectives to form adverbs.

What you need

Copies of *The Twits*.

What to do

- Ask the children to identify the common element in these words: softly, sadly, anxiously, slowly, gently, wisely. (The suffix 'ly'.) Ask: *What is the root word in each case?* (Soft, sad, anxious, slow, gentle, wise.) Do they notice the root words are all adjectives? Explain that adding 'ly' changes an adjective into an adverb to describe the action, not the person.

- Show the children the illustrations of Mr and Mrs Twit (inside the front cover) and use adverbs to describe their behaviour. For example: Mr Twit behaves badly (not Mr Twit is bad); Mrs Twit speaks rudely to others (not Mrs Twit is rude). One describes the noun, the other the action.

- Orally, complete some sentences changing the adjective to an adverb by adding 'ly': 'The Twits behave bad (badly).' 'The children ran home quick (quickly).' 'The monkeys laughed loud (loudly).' 'The birds flew quiet (quietly) past the tree.' 'Mr Twit eager (eagerly) catches birds.'

- Encourage the children to write their own sentences to describe the behaviour of different characters in the story.

Differentiation

Support: Ask children to find sentences in the book containing adverbs. Provide extra words to give them practice (smug/smugly, cruel/cruelly). Let them use a dictionary to check their spelling.

Extension: Invite children to make up rules to explain the spelling in these words: careful – carefully; gentle – gently; dramatic – dramatically; true – truly; happy – happily.

3. Look who's talking!

Objective

To introduce inverted commas to punctuate direct speech.

What you need

Extract 2, highlighters or pens, printable pages 'Introducing inverted commas' and 'Writing frame', interactive activity 'Mark my words'.

What to do

- Check that all the children understand the terms 'direct speech' and 'dialogue'. Direct speech refers to the words that a person actually says; dialogue is a conversation.

- Read Extract 2 together. Ask the children to find the direct speech and use different-coloured pens or highlighters for each character.

- Now choose volunteers to re-read the text 'in character'. The characters read the highlighted parts and the narrator reads the rest.

- Explain that inverted commas are necessary punctuation marks. Ask: *What purpose do inverted commas serve?* (They mark out the direct speech of each character.) *How do they help the reader?* (They help the reader make sense of the text.)

- Hand out printable page 'Introducing inverted commas' and 'Writing frame' for the children to complete. They should first make up a comic strip showing characters with speech bubbles, and then write out the conversation in direct speech. (The 'Writing frame' sheet can be used as a guide to mark out direct speech.) Remind them to start a new line for each speaker.

- Encourage the children to write a short dialogue to add to the story, using an existing scene or a new scene (such as another trick). The scene should unfold through the dialogue.

Differentiation

Support: Let children copy a short dialogue from the book to practise the punctuation.
Extension: Let children complete interactive activity 'Mark my words' for further practice.

4. That apostrophe is mine

Objective

To use apostrophes with singular and plural nouns to indicate possession.

What you need

Copies of *The Twits*, photocopiable page 23 'My apostrophe'.

What to do

- Test the children's prior knowledge. Ask: *When do we use an apostrophe to show possession* (when something belongs to someone or something) *or omission* (in contractions to show where letters have been omitted)? Find examples in the text.

- A common error is children over-using the apostrophe and adding it to any word ending in an 's'. Use examples to make it clear. The possessive noun is followed by a noun:
  - Plural: *The Twits were mean and smelly.* Possession: *Mr Twit's house has no windows.*
  - Plural: *The monkeys laughed loudly.* Possession: *The monkey's cage is small.*
  - Plural: *The boys were stuck in the tree.* Possession: *The boy's pants were left behind.*
  - Plural: *The birds were cooked.* Possession: *The bird's feet got stuck onto the tree.*

- Now show how the apostrophe's position changes if the owner is a plural noun. Use the previous sentences to demonstrate the apostrophe before the 's' for singular, but after the 's' for plural: The Twits' house; The monkeys' cage; The boys' pants; The birds' feet.

- Provide the children with photocopiable page 23 and ask them to complete it independently.

Differentiation

Support: Give children sentences containing possessive nouns and ask them to fill in the apostrophe.
Extension: Invite these children to find out what happens if the owner is already plural in form, such as *children, men, mice, geese.* (Add apostrophe plus 's'.)

5. Adverbials move up

Objective

To use fronted adverbials to sequence events.

What you need

Printable page 'Mix 'n' match', dry macaroni.

What to do

- Ask: *What do adverbials do in a sentence?* (Expand it, make it flow, provide extra information about time, manner and place. For example: Later that day (time)/Quickly (manner)/Back on the ground (place), the boys ran home.) Adverbials also show the order of events, such as: **First**, he fetched the balloons. **Then**, he filled them with gas.

- Explain that adverbials can move around in a sentence. When placed at the beginning of a sentence, they are called fronted adverbials and are followed by a comma to indicate a slight pause and to separate the phrase from the main clause.

- Using photocopiable page 'Mix 'n' match', ask the children to cut out the sentence cards and mix and match their own sentences. They can move their sentence cards around to show fronted adverbials and place macaroni pieces where the comma should go. Invite children to share their sentences with the rest of the class. You may want to enlarge the page to A3.

- Using fronted adverbials, invite the children to summarise one of the tricks from the story showing the sequence of events. Each trick can be summarised in four or five steps.

Differentiation

Support: Give the children a mixed-up sequence of events to order correctly using the fronted adverbials as clues.

Extension: Choose an event from the story and write a lead sentence for a newspaper report describing the event. Begin with a fronted adverbial such as *Early yesterday morning, four little boys were discovered stuck to a tree.* Write as many lead sentences as you like.

6. Words have families too

Objective

To explore word families showing common words related in form and meaning.

What you need

Copies of *The Twits,* photocopiable page 24 'Word families'.

What to do

- Discuss the idea of family units where everyone is connected and shares a common bond.

- Tell the children that words also belong in word families. Test their prior knowledge. Ask: *Can you explain how words can be related to each other?* Ask for some examples.

- Explain that when you change words, the function of the word may change but it still belongs in the same family – for example, 'hair', 'hairy', 'hairdryer'. Adjectives of comparison are part of the same family: 'dirty', 'dirtier', 'dirtiest'. Participles and verb endings also form part of the same word family: 'walking', 'walks', 'walker', 'walked'. Use examples from the dictionary to demonstrate – for example, 'horrid', 'horror', 'horrific', 'horrendous'.

- Ask the children to imagine that the Twits have a family with children and pets. Discuss word families to describe this family. For example: 'Mr Twit is horrid, Mrs Twit is horrible, Baby Twit is a horror and the pet dog is horrific.'

- Ask the children to complete photocopiable page 24 'Word families', using dictionaries to help them find as many related words as possible.

Differentiation

Support: Revise using comparative adjectives to describe other characters and objects in the story. For example: The monkeys: 'small', 'smaller', 'smallest'; the house: 'dark', 'darker', 'darkest'.

Extension: Invite children to repeat the activity on the photocopiable sheet, this time using root words that belong to the monkey family, such as 'friend', 'sad', 'clever', 'help', 'free'.

Picky prefixes

● Mr Twit is not the cleanest person around! Add the prefix 'un' to six of the words shown below to correctly describe Mr Twit's beard.

attractive   clean

messy   hygienic

combed   scruffy

healthy   tidy

awful   dirty

● Help Mr Twit stick the correct prefixes to each of the following words to make them mean the opposite. Write them in the correct glue pot.

agreeable   willing   happy   patient   social   tasteful
loving   kind   obedient   polite   satisfied

dis   un   im   anti

My apostrophe

● Use the words below to complete the labels to show who owns what. Don't forget to fill in the missing apostrophe!

> pot of glue   glass eye   trousers   feather   cage   pond

Mrs Twit
_____

Mr Twit
_____

Muggle-Wumps
_____

The birds
_____

The boys
_____

The frogs
_____

● Circle the correct word in each sentence to show that the owner is a plural.

1. The Twits / Twit's / Twits' house was dark and cold.

2. The monkey's / monkeys' / monkeys cage was small.

3. The tree's / trees / trees' branches had no leaves.

4. The birds / bird's / birds' friends tried to warn them.

5. The little boy's / boys' / boys pants were left behind.

6. The plants / plant's / plants' thorns were prickly.

Word families

● Help this dead tree to grow again by adding new words to it. Use a dictionary to find more words related to each root word shown below.

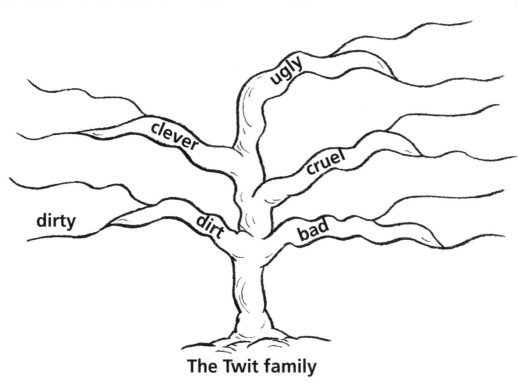

The Twit family

● Sort out your words to show which ones belong to which grammar family. Complete the frames with as many words as you can.

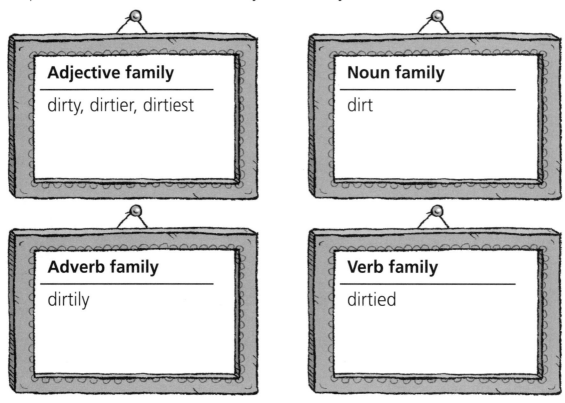

Adjective family

dirty, dirtier, dirtiest

Noun family

dirt

Adverb family

dirtily

Verb family

dirtied

1. First impressions

Objective

To introduce characters and write a character profile.

What you need

Copies of *The Twits*, media resource 'Men with beards', printable page 'Food word search'.

What to do

- Display these words on the board: friendly, jovial, wise, important, old, adventurous, mean, mysterious, wild, intelligent. Display the images on media resource 'Men with beards'. Match the words provided with the person – for example, Santa Claus has a big curly, white beard that makes him look friendly and jovial.

- Now read aloud chapters 1–3 of the book. Then ask: *Why does Mr Twit have a beard?* (He thinks it makes him look 'wise and grand'.) *What can be found in his beard? Why does the author go into such detail about Mr Twit's appearance, particularly his beard?* (It gives the reader insight into the type of person he is and it sets the scene for what's to come.) *Would you like to meet Mr Twit? Why/Why not? Do you think he might change in the story?*

- Ask the children to start a character profile to record their first impressions of each character they meet in the book, using the headings: Physical appearance, Behaviour, Character traits. At the end of the story they can look back to see if the character changed.

- Invite the children to use their character profiles to introduce a story character to the class. Ask: *How would you introduce your character?* (For example: This is Mr Twit. He has a very thick beard of which he is very proud...)

Differentiation

Support: Invite children to complete printable page 'Food word search'.
Extension: Encourage children to research famous people with beards, and to present them to the rest of the class.

2. Villains wanted

Objective

To use simple organisational devices to create a poster.

What you need

Copies of *The Twits*, media resource 'Wanted poster', interactive activity 'Villains wanted'.

What to do

- Explain to the class that most stories have both villains and heroes. The hero (protagonist) is the main good character who you'd like to see defeat the villain and be happy. The villain (or antagonist) is the main bad character who tries to prevent the hero from being happy.

- On a sheet of paper, ask the children to make two columns with the headings 'heroes' and 'villains' and to place the story's main characters into one or other column. Discuss their answers. Which names did they put where, and why?

- Tell the class that if the police are looking for someone, they often publish a 'wanted' poster which asks members of the public to help identify the person. Display the media resource 'Wanted poster' and ask: *What features does the poster have?* (A heading, a picture.) *What is missing?* (Other relevant information.)

- Next, open the interactive activity 'Villains wanted'. In pairs, children can take turns describing a character from the story for their partner to draw, using the interactive drawing tools. On screen 2 they can design a 'Wanted' poster for Mr or Mrs Twit using the headings provided. Remind them to use appropriate adjectives, pronouns and correct spelling and punctuation. Encourage the use of dictionaries and thesauruses to develop vocabulary.

Differentiation

Support: Provide sentence starters in each section to aid less confident learners.
Extension: Invite children to choose another character from the story and create a 'missing' poster such as 'Missing monkeys' 'Missing boys' or 'Missing couple'.

3. Job opportunities

Objective

To read and write for real purposes.

What you need

Job-finder section of a local newspaper or magazine, photocopiable page 29 'Character job finder', interactive activity 'Job application form'.

Cross-curricular link

Citizenship

What to do

- Go through the job finder section of your local newspaper. Read out some of the jobs advertised with their descriptions. What information do they request? What skills do different jobs require?

- Ask: *What are the characters in the story 'good' at?* (Mr Twit – catching birds and telling lies; Mrs Twit – making bird pie, growing certain plants and talking loudly; monkeys – circus tricks and making plans, Roly-Poly Bird – helping out; the little boys – climbing trees, running fast!)

- Invite the children to match the skills of each character with jobs they would be good at – for example, Mrs Twit could be a baker or chef, or she could grow and sell thistles, and stinging nettles.

- In small groups, ask the children to work through photocopiable page 29 'Character job finder'. Encourage creative answers. Share answers and discuss good ideas.

- Once they have finished the photocopiable sheet, ask the children to complete the interactive activity 'Job application form' independently. Emphasise the importance of accurate answers when filling in forms.

Differentiation

Extension: Encourage children to explore other types of forms and how to complete them. If possible, get hold of a library or school application and let them practise filling it in.

4. Test the plot

Objective

To sequence and summarise the plot in narratives.

What you need

Copies of *The Twits*, interactive activity 'Sequence it', photocopiable page 30 'Test the plot'.

What to do

- Open the interactive activity 'Sequence it' and let the children move the events into the correct order. Revise 'before' and 'after' (for example, the frog trick came **before** the worms and **after** the glass eye trick).

- Explain to the children that every story has a plot; it is how the events in the story are sequenced. The first part, the exposition, is usually background information about the characters and setting. Ask: *What background does the author give about the Twits?* (What they look like and their behaviour.) *What can we understand from this?* (They are the story's 'villains'.)

- The next part of the plot introduces the conflict, which describes the problems faced by the characters. The reader is left wondering how these problems will be solved. Ask: *What problem do the animals face?* (The Twits mistreat them.)

- The climax is where things begin to change in the story, when the villain is defeated or the hero is triumphant.

- The resolution ends the story and explains what happens to the characters after the climax.

- Ask: *Does Roald Dahl's story fit the plot pattern? Let's put it to the test.* Ask the children to use photocopiable page 30 'Test the plot' to summarise the main events in the story.

Differentiation

Support: Ask children to summarise one part of the plot in a short comic strip.

Extension: Ask children to change one part of the plot (such as the problem or the climax) and summarise it in a comic strip.

5. A sticky end

Objective

To change the plot in narratives.

What you need

Copies of *The Twits*, printable page 'Storyboard template'.

What to do

- With the class, read the last few chapters of the book. Ask: *What do you feel about the ending? Did you expect it to end this way? Is it a satisfactory end? Why?*

- Ask the children to list the characters and recount what happens to each one in the end. Ask for their opinions: *Does each character receive a just reward? In life, do the heroes always win? Should bad things happen to bad people and good things happen to good people? Should people be punished if they do bad things? Is it right that Mr and Mrs Twit were punished equally? Did the punishment fit the crime? Can you think of another way to punish them?*

- In small groups, discuss other ways the story could have ended. Ask: *If you could rewrite the end, what would you change? Would you change the hero of the story?* Share ideas.

- In groups, plan a new ending from the chapter 'Muggle-Wump Has an Idea'. Hand out copies of printable page 'Storyboard template' for the children to complete, showing a different way to end the tale. For each of the six steps they should describe (or draw) an event, adding some dialogue below.

- Once they have completed their sheets, invite each group to present their storyboards to the rest of the class. Take a class vote on their favourite ending.

Differentiation

Extension: Encourage children to write the new ending in typical Roald Dahl style.

6. Show what you know

Objective

To develop understanding of what they read.

What you need

Copies of *The Twits*, photocopiable page 31 'Reading comprehension', interactive activity 'True or false?'.

What to do

- Discuss the climax of the story. Ask: *Where does the reader begin to see a change of direction in the story?* (Chapters 22–26.) *How can you tell that things are changing?* (The animals begin to carry out a plan of revenge.)

- Together with the class, read the chapter 'The Carpet Goes on the Ceiling'. Next, pose some true or false statements to find out if the children paid attention to the story: All the animals got involved in the revenge plan (T); The Roly-Poly Bird had the idea first (F); The little monkeys thought the plan was impossible (T); The animals had lots of time to put their plan into action (F).

- Let the children answer further true/false questions in the interactive activity 'True or false?'.

- Now get the children to work in pairs. They can take turns to make up questions for each other, based on different parts of the plot, such as the exposition, the conflict, the climax or the resolution. Tell them that once they've had time to practise their question-and-answer skills they will answer questions based on chapter 24 as it is part of the climax.

- Hand out copies of photocopiable page 31 'Reading comprehension' and ask the children to answer the questions independently. Set a time limit for this. (The questions have been designed to address different levels of understanding.)

Differentiation

Support: Make sure the children understand the text and the questions before they start work on the photocopiable sheet.

7. Who said what?

Objective
To role play dialogue.

What you need
Copies of *The Twits*, interactive activity 'Quiz: who said what?'.

What to do

- Conduct a 'Who said it?' quiz with the class. Read some dialogue from different parts of the story and ask the children if they can guess which character said it.

- Remind the children that dialogue is used to show character development and help unfold the plot.

- As additional reinforcement for this activity, open the interactive activity 'Quiz: who said what?' and ask the children to complete it.

- Look at parts of the book without dialogue. Ask: *Why isn't there dialogue?* (Dialogue isn't always necessary especially if the author is describing a person or setting.)

- Ask the children to identify places in the story where dialogue could be added. For example, Mr and Mrs Twit talking about what to put in the bird pie; one boy explaining to his mum what happened to them; the monkeys discussing how awful life is in a cage.

- Let the children work in pairs or groups to develop a new dialogue. Give them time to invent and practise the new dialogue. Encourage impromptu speech because it is time-consuming to write the dialogue down and learn it.

- Finally, invite pairs to act out their dialogues for the rest of the class.

Differentiation
Support: Let the children choose a short dialogue from the story and practise it as is.
Extension: Invite children to develop a phone conversation between two imaginary characters, such as two neighbours discussing what they've seen and heard.

8. House for sale

Objective
To give well-structured descriptions for different purposes.

What you need
Copies of *The Twits*, media resources 'Different homes' and 'House for sale', printable page 'Scan the setting'.

What to do

- Show the children the images of different houses in media resource 'Different homes'. For each house, ask them if they would like to live there, and why it does or does not appeal.

- Together, read the chapters 'The House, the Tree and the Monkey Cage' and 'The Roly-Poly Bird to the Rescue'. Ask: *Why is the setting in a story important?* (It informs the reader when and where the story takes place and provides a backdrop and context to the story.)

- Hand out printable page 'Scan the setting'. Ask the children to circle words that match the descriptions in the story. Can they imagine the house inside?

- Now open media resource 'House for sale'. Ask: *If the Twit's house was for sale, what positive words could you use to describe it? What catchy slogan would fit?* (Deal of the day! Perfect house to fix-up!) *Are there any other features that could be mentioned positively?* (Has a garden that takes care of itself; a secure house with only one entrance; sound-proof, very private.)

- Discuss how to make something sound positive using persuasive language. Let the children practise 'selling' the Twits' house to a partner before asking them to design a 'For sale' advertisement.

Differentiation
Support: Help children make a collage of catchy slogans and advertisements for houses.
Extension: Ask children to write a 'For sale' advertisement for a house from a different story (for example, the gingerbread house in the story of *Hansel and Gretel*).

Character job finder

- The characters in the story are all good at something, even Mr Twit! Help each one find a job to suit their character and skills.
- List their character traits, their skills and the jobs they might be good at in the spaces below.

Mr Twit	Character traits:
	Skills:
	Occupation:

Mrs Twit	Character traits:
	Skills:
	Occupation:

Muggle-Wump	Character traits:
	Skills:
	Occupation:

Roly-Poly Bird	Character traits:
	Skills:
	Occupation:

Test the plot

The plot is how the main events in the story unfold.
● Make notes in the second column below summarising what happens in each part of the plot of *The Twits*.

Exposition (Introduction)	Describe the main characters and setting.
Conflict (Problem)	What problem are the animals faced with?
Climax (Point at which things change)	Describe the turning point.
Resolution (Ending)	What happens to all the characters in the end?

Reading comprehension

● Read the chapter 'The Carpet Goes on the Ceiling' in *The Twits*, then answer these questions.

1. What is 'The greatest upside-down trick of all time'?

_____

2. What do these expressions mean:

   'Give me a hand.' _____

   'Poor old muggles has gone off his wump.' _____

   'You nitwits.' _____

3. Who thought the job was impossible?

_____

4. Find five synonyms for the word 'said' in the text.

_____   _____   _____   _____   _____

5. Describe the size and colour of the carpet using four adjectives from the text.

_____   _____   _____   _____

6. Write T (true) or F (false) next to these statements:

   The animals thought the job was impossible. _____

   Muggle-Wump was in a hurry. _____

   The carpet covered the entire ceiling from wall to wall. _____

   The carpet was easy to move. _____

   All the animals helped. _____

7. Why did Muggle-Wump want the carpet on the ceiling?

_____

8. Do you think it was a good plan? Why?

_____

▼ TALK ABOUT IT

1. Glue for sale!

Objective

To participate in presentations.

What you need

Copies of *The Twits*, printable pages 'Words that stick' and 'Comparative adjectives'.

Cross-curricular link

Science

What to do

• Read the chapter 'Hugtight Sticky Glue' together and ask: *What qualities does the glue have? What did Mr Twit use it for? Why is HUGTIGHT a good glue name?* (HUGTIGHT implies the glue is strong and sticks firmly.)

• Let the children note names of some products they use – toothpaste, soap, snacks, drinks and so on. *What purpose do the names serve?* (To catch attention, give clues on what it does, advertise it.)

• Explain that 'HUGTIGHT' is an invented compound word made from the words 'hug' and 'tight'. Invite the children to invent other names for glue using compound words (Stickfast, Holdon, Neverfail). Then ask them to complete printable page 'Words that stick'.

• Explain to the children that adjectives of comparison are useful for comparing things with another. They are used to compare two (comparative adjectives 'er') or more (superlative adjectives 'est') things. Hand out printable page 'Comparative adjectives' for the children to complete.

• Finally, ask them to work in pairs to prepare a short oral presentation to advertise their glue. It should catch the audience's attention with an interesting name and slogan (encourage the use of superlative adjectives!), and be loud and clear for all to hear.

Differentiation

Support: Help children to make up a jingle or ditty to go with the advertisement.
Extension: Ask children to advertise Mr Twit's upside-down circus or Mrs Twit's Bird Pie.

2. Act it out

Objective

To participate in role play.

What you need

Copies of *The Twits*, printable page 'Monkey teamwork tips'.

What to do

• Group work can be challenging. Hand out printable page 'Monkey teamwork tips' and use it to prepare the children to work together.

• Ask the children to identify their favourite parts from the story taking turns to read the best bits aloud from the book. Ask: *Would some parts be more fun to act than others? Why?*

• In small groups, invite the children to choose a scene and create a frozen moment (tableau). Using facial expression, body language and position they should show a moment in the story, as if a photograph had been taken.

• Now ask the groups to choose another scene, and this time to mime it. Once again, they must rely on facial expressions and movements only to perform the scene. Invite the rest of the class to try to identify which scene from the book is being enacted.

• Once the groups are working well, they can move on to the final role-play activity and choose one of these topics to enact: a new scene (such as a new trick or Mr and Mrs Twit going shopping); a situation where they meet Mr and Mrs Twit or playing a trick on a friend and the consequences.

• If time permits, let the groups perform their role plays for the class, using dressing-up clothes or simple props if appropriate.

Differentiation

Support: Ask children to write out some rules for acting out a scene (for example, speak clearly).
Extension: Invite children to perform a monologue – be one character and say what you really think and feel about an event in the story.

3. Don't judge a book by its cover

Objective

To participate in discussions.

What you need

Copies of *The Twits*, photocopiable page 35 'Stereotypes', printable page 'Monkey teamwork tips'.

Cross-curricular link

Citizenship

What to do

- Together, come up with some 'rules for discussions' (such as only one person should speak at a time) and display them on the board.

- Demonstrate how people don't always agree. Ask the children to indicate by show of hands who agrees or disagrees with statements such as: It's OK to keep monkeys in cages; little children who trespass should be punished; it's OK to eat bird pie; bad people are ugly.

- Explain that a stereotype is a fixed idea people have about what a particular type of person is like, even if that idea is wrong. Point out that Roald Dahl is known for exaggerating his characters and using stereotypes to enhance his stories. Refer to a picture of the Twits in the book. Ask: *Why are the Twits stereotypes?* (They are mean and cruel. Their ugly, dirty appearance mirrors their bad nature.)

- Organise the children into groups. Provide each group with photocopiable page 35 'Stereotypes'. Ask them to discuss the questions on the sheet and note down their responses. Use printable page 'Monkey teamwork tips' to guide group work.

- Finally, invite each group to report back to the rest of the class on their findings.

Differentiation

Support: Ask children to identify stereotypical characters from fairytales and folk stories (for example, the 'Big Bad Wolf').

Extension: Invite children to discuss other topics such as: Is it OK/not OK to use stereotypes in jokes?

4. Answer the question!

Objective

To use spoken language to develop understanding.

What you need

Copies of *The Twits*, photocopiable page 36 'Interview role play', media resource 'Monkey in a cage'.

What to do

- Explain to the class that an interview is a way of finding out about another person and getting information from their experience. Ask: *Who does interviews?* (Reporters, talk show hosts, researchers, detectives and so on.)

- Together, read aloud the chapter 'The Great Upside-Down Monkey Circus' and the first part of the next chapter, 'The Roly-Poly Bird to the Rescue'.

- Now tell the children to imagine being an investigator who is responding to a complaint about the monkeys being mistreated. Open media resource 'Monkey in a cage' and ask them to think of some questions they would ask Muggle-Wump, using the present tense. For example: Why are you in a cage? Do you enjoy it? How does it make you feel? How long must you practise every day? What would you like to do instead? What happens if you don't listen? How do you feel about the Twits?

- Explain that if you interview someone you will get just one side of the story, so imagine interviewing Mr Twit to get **his** side of the story! What would he say? Provide each child with photocopiable page 36 'Interview role play' and ask them to complete it.

- Choose children to represent different characters in the story. They can role play interviewing different characters about the same event – for example, interview both Mr and Mrs Twit and a witness to get all views about the stretching incident.

Differentiation

Extension: Invite more confident children to conduct impromptu interviews where they don't get time to prepare or practise.

5. Speak up

Objective

To speak audibly and fluently.

What you need

Photocopiable page 37 'Prepare to speak!'.

What to do

- Explain to the children that they are going to give a presentation in character. They will plan, prepare and practise a presentation on one of the following topics:
  - Mrs Twit: Making the perfect meal for Mr Twit
  - Muggle-Wump: Taking care of your pets
  - Roly-Poly Bird: Travelling to Africa – what to pack and places to visit
  - Mr Twit: The do's and don'ts of tricking your friends and family
  - Health officer: Taking care of yourself – useful hygiene tips for the Twits.

- Some of these topics will require research and others imagination. Tell the children that they should choose a topic according to the level of research they are able to do.

- Use photocopiable page 37 'Prepare to speak!' to guide the planning. A presentation should have a structure. The introduction should explain what the presentation is about and grab the audience's attention, for example by an interesting statement, a quote or asking a question (for example, 'When last did you enjoy a good Bird Pie?'). The body should be organised and ordered as separate points, especially if there are instructions. The conclusion should sum up the presentation. A presentation should be well-planned and practised.

- Discuss criteria such as structure, eye contact, and vocal and facial expression. Display these criteria on the board. After each presentation, discuss with the class which criteria were missing or done well.

Differentiation

Support: Help children prepare speech cards showing the main points and key words.
Extension: Invite children to adapt their presentations for a younger audience.

6. Can I persuade you?

Objective

To articulate and justify opinions.

What you need

Printable page 'All about beards'.

Cross-curricular link

Citizenship

What to do

- Tell the children that Roald Dahl didn't like beards and apparently this inspired him to write this story. Ask: *Do you have any unusual dislikes?*

- Many famous historical characters had beards and today there are ordinary people and famous people with beards. Use the information provided on printable page 'All about beards' to have a discussion on the role and history of beards.

- Now invite the children to imagine trying to persuade Roald Dahl that beards are not actually that bad. Working in groups, ask them to draw up a list all the reasons why beards are great. They should practise persuasive phrases such as: 'We believe…' 'Based on popular opinion…' 'Consider that…' 'It is clear that…'.

- When the groups have prepared their statements, invite them to report back to the rest of the class.

- Other topics from the story that can be used to practise persuasive speech are:
  - Mr Twit: A house with no windows is better than a house with windows…
  - Muggle-Wump: Animals should not be kept in cages…
  - One of the little boys stuck in the tree: Children should not be punished…
  - Mr Twit: I'm really not so bad…

Differentiation

Support: Encourage children to use persuasive devices such as adverbs of degree in their statements (very, really, extremely, hardly…).
Extension: Ask more confident children to prepare and present their own persuasive speech.

Stereotypes

● Which statements do you think are stereotypes and why?

People with glasses are clever.

_____

_____

Baby brothers are annoying.

_____

_____

Girls have long hair.

_____

_____

● Do you think a 'stereotype' is a positive or negative thing? Why?

_____

_____

_____

● Circle the best option in each sentence. According to the stereotype:

A clown is funny / serious.   A crook is bad / good.

A hero is kind / mean.   A pirate is dirty / clean.

Grandmothers are young / old.   A king is rich / poor.

● In the story of _The Twits_, is Muggle-Wump your idea of a hero? Why?

_____

_____

_____

Interview role play

The Twits have been reported for animal cruelty and disturbing the peace.
You are the police officer investigating and you interview everyone involved.

● Find out both sides of the story. Fill in possible answers and then role play the interview with a partner.

Interviewer	Muggle-Wump
How does Mr Twit treat you?	
What do you think of Mr Twit?	
How could he improve your situation?	
Interviewer	**Mr Twit**
Why do you keep monkeys in a cage?	
How well do you look after them?	
What could you do to improve their situation?	

● Choose another character from the story and write your own questions to ask. Fill in possible answers giving their point of view. Role play the interview with a partner.

Interviewer	First character

Prepare to speak!

Mrs Twit is not used to speaking in front of an audience. Help her by showing her what to do.

● List important presentation tips she should know (the first one has already been done for you).

Face the audience

Mrs Twit

● Help Mrs Twit to plan her presentation on the topic below.

Topic: Making the perfect meal for Mr Twit
Introduction:
Body (steps to follow): 1. 2. 3.
Conclusion:

GET WRITING

1. Instructions 1-2-3

To use simple organisational devices when writing.

Copies of *The Twits*, photocopiable page 41 'Sticky instructions', printable page 'Give the command'.

What to do

- Refer to photocopiable page 41 'Sticky instructions' on how to make glue. Ask: *What type of text is this?* (Instructional.) *How can you tell?* (Headings, ordered steps, command verbs, fronted adverbials.) Underline the command verbs – the verbs at the beginning of each step. Ask: *When you use a command verb, what part of the sentence is missing?* (The subject – you – has been left out.)

- Ask: *In what other situations do you follow instructions?* (Games, recipes, directions.)

- Together, read the chapter 'Mrs Twit Gets a Stretching'. Ask the children to list all the things Mr Twit used. Identify the order in which he worked. Identify the action words.

- Work together to change the text into a set of instructions: How to Stretch Mrs Twit. (Equipment: 100 balloons, lots of string, gas cylinder, iron ring. Method: Fix an iron ring into the ground; Tie Mrs Twit's ankles to the iron ring; Fill the balloons with gas, one at a time…)

- The Twits were good at making up awful tricks to play on others. Invite the children to choose one of these tricks and write their own instructions. Tell them to set out the instructions in a format similar to 'Sticky instructions', and to use headings and ordered steps.

Support: Let the children complete photocopiable page 'Give the command' to revise command verbs and writing instructions.

Extension: Ask children to write recipes for meals such as bird pie, wormy spaghetti or minced chicken livers on toast.

2. Monkey facts

To retrieve and record information.

Copies of *The Twits*, photocopiable page 42 'All about monkeys', media resource 'Gecko factfile', interactive activity 'Key words'.

What to do

- Read aloud the chapters 'The Great Upside-Down Monkey Circus', 'The Roly-Poly Bird to the Rescue' and 'The Monkeys Escape'. Encourage the children to listen for specific information about the monkeys.

- Ask: *Where could you look to find more information on monkeys?* (Reference books, nature programmes, internet…) *When researching an animal, what questions should you ask?* (Where does it live? What does it eat? and so on.)

- Highlight the importance of finding facts. Ask: *How can you tell if something is a fact or an opinion?* (A fact is something that can be proved. An opinion is what someone thinks or believes.)

- Ask the children to complete photocopiable page 42 'All about monkeys' in which they need to identify whether various statements are facts or opinions. The second part of the sheet asks them to read through the text again and underline the key words in all the factual statements (the most important nouns, verbs and some important adjectives).

- Finally, invite the children to design a monkey factfile to summarise and display the information under headings. As a guide, show them the media resource 'Gecko factfile' and identify the headings and key words. Ask: *How many facts can you remember without looking? Which are your favourite facts?*

Support: Help children to identify key words in the text about glue on the interactive activity 'Key words'.

Extension: Invite children to design a factfile for a story character, as a type of book review.

3. Time to rhyme

Objective

To prepare poems to read and perform.

What you need

Copies of *The Twits*, examples of traditional rhymes, media resource 'The Roly-Poly Bird's rhyme'.

Cross-curricular link

Citizenship

What to do

- Talk about rhymes. Ask: *What rhymes do you know? Can you repeat them? When are rhymes used?* (Sing, advertise, remember something.)

- With the class, read aloud the two verses shown on the media resource 'The Roly-Poly Bird's rhyme'. Analyse the form of the rhyme. Ask: *Which words rhyme?* (Tree/free, high/pie.) *What is the rhyme scheme?* (AABB.) *How many lines are in each stanza?* (Four.) *Which lines or phrases are repeated?* (The last two lines.)

- Working in pairs or small groups, invite the children to make up another stanza for this rhyme. First, the birds respond to the Roly-Poly Bird. The children should change the words to be in the first person. Give an example: There's sticky stuff on our feet and the tree / If we stay here longer we'll never be free / We'll fly away! Fly away! Stay up high! / So we don't finish up in a hot Bird Pie!

- Now encourage the children to come up with another stanza on their own. They can choose to be the Roly-Poly Bird or one of the other birds responding.

- Once they have four stanzas, let the groups prepare and present the whole rhyme to the class.

Differentiation

Support: Provide adult support if necessary to help children prepare their rhymes.
Extension: Invite children to adapt an existing rhyme or song to make up a rhyme about the Twits.

4. Be wise, advertise!

Objective

To plan, discuss and record ideas for creative writing.

What you need

Examples of relevant age-appropriate advertisements.

What to do

- Show the children examples of various posters and advertisements for products, shows, films or books. Discuss different persuasive devices and ways the writer gets the reader's attention, such as alliteration, clear print, bold statements, strong vocabulary, figurative language, appeals to the reader's emotions or sense of humour. Look for examples of these in the advertisements.

- As a class, think of how you might advertise something you are all familiar with (for example, the school). Discuss words and phrases you could use. Look for opportunities to include alliteration, humour, figurative language and so on.

- Next, invite pairs of children to design an advertisement for one of the following: The school stage production of *The Twits*, the first Great Upside-Down Monkey Circus, Mrs Twit's Bird Pie, Hairy Beard Shampoo.

- Ask the pairs to talk through ideas first. Encourage them to use interesting adjectives. They should draw a picture to go with the advertisement and use other graphics to appeal to their readers.

- Remind the children of the writing process – plan, draft, edit, proofread and amend.

Differentiation

Support: Ask children to draw up guidelines of things to include in advertisements (for example, catchy names and slogans).
Extension: Link this task to the oral advertisement for HUGTIGHT glue (see activity on page 32). The children can adapt it and use their ideas to create a poster.

5. Read all about it

Objective
To write for real purposes.

What you need
Copies of *The Twits*, examples of local news reports, photocopiable page 43 'News report', printable page 'Writing frame', poster paper.

Cross-curricular link
Citizenship

What to do

- Write these headlines on the board: Woman seen ballooning into the sky; Little boys tell of ordeal; Animal cruelty case suspect disappears. Ask the children to identify each event from the story of *The Twits*.

- Show the class some examples of newspaper stories with eye-catching headlines. Discuss how headlines get the reader's attention and summarise an event.

- Explain that news reports provide current information on 'who', 'what', 'when', 'where' and 'why' or 'how' something happened. Ask: *What else does a news report have?* (Photo(s), quotations, witness accounts, different points of view, facts and opinions.)

- In groups, pairs or individually, invite the children to choose one event in the story of *The Twits*, and write a news report.

- Let them use photocopiable page 43 'News report' to plan their report. Information can be adapted from the story, and some can be imagined. Encourage the children to be creative and add in extra relevant information, such as an account from a witness. They can invent at least one quote, using inverted commas (provide them with printable page 'Writing frame' to refer to if necessary).

- After planning, the children should take time to edit their work using dictionaries.

- Provide poster paper for the children to make a neat copy of their final work. Display the completed versions around the classroom.

6. Once upon a time...

Objective
To draft, write and present narratives.

What you need
Examples of well-known fairy tales, printable page 'Storyboard template'.

What to do

- Explain to the class that most stories have a similar plot. Organise the children into small groups and ask them to identify the plot in some familiar fairy stories. Ask: *Apart from the plot, what other elements and themes do fairy stories have in common with each other?* (A magical object or person such as a witch or fairy godmother, the triumph of good over evil.) *Is the story of* The Twits *a fairy tale? Why/why not?* (No. Typical fairy story elements are missing.)

- Encourage the children to discuss ideas for how to turn the story of *The Twits* into a fairy tale. What magical objects or people could they introduce? (For example, a magic paint brush, a flying carpet, a fairy godmother, a talking mirror on the wall, a house of sweets, magic beans…)

- Working independently, invite the children to choose one part (beginning, middle or end) of the story to retell as a fairy story. Provide them with copies of printable page 'Storyboard template' and ask them to show, in six steps, how to tell the story as a fairy tale.

- They should write it with dialogue. Remind them to edit and check their punctuation and spelling.

- Once their stories are neatly written out, let them take turns to read it aloud to the class, using vocal and facial expression. If possible, find a younger audience to entertain.

Differentiation

Support: Let children focus on one chapter of the story only.
Extension: Encourage children to turn the fairy tale into a cartoon.

Sticky instructions

- Read the instructions below and complete these tasks:
  - Underline the headings.
  - Number the steps.
  - Circle the command verbs at the start of each step.
  - Fill in the missing items in 'Things you need'.
  - Add these adverbials: To begin, next, then, finally.

How to make home-made glue

Here is a great way to make your own glue to stick things together. Remember to handle glue with care!

Things you need

1 cup flour

$\frac{1}{3}$ cup sugar

$1\frac{1}{2}$ cups water (approximately)

1 tsp vinegar

_____

_____

_____

Method

_____ Place all the ingredients together in a pot.

_____ Stir the mixture with a wooden spoon. Keep stirring.

_____ Ask an adult to help you with the next step.

_____ Warm up the mixture on a hot stove until it thickens.

_____ Turn the stove off and wait for it to cool.

_____ Use it! See what things it can stick together.

All about monkeys

- Write F or O in the boxes next to each statement to show which statements about monkeys are facts (F), and which are opinions (O).

☐ Monkeys are interesting creatures.

☐ Monkeys are mammals of the primate order.

☐ Monkeys love doing tricks and entertaining people.

☐ A group of monkeys is called a troop.

☐ Keeping monkeys as pets is cruel.

☐ Monkeys can grasp with their hands and feet.

☐ Baby monkeys are cared for by the mother for a long time.

☐ Baby monkeys are cute.

☐ Monkeys are not apes.

☐ Monkeys live in tropical forests, grasslands and mountains.

☐ Most monkeys are omnivorous – they eat animals and plants.

☐ Monkeys like bananas.

- Now you know which statements are facts, circle the key words in the factual statements. (You don't need to circle the word 'monkey' each time because it is the topic.)

News report

- Imagine you are a news reporter. Choose an unusual, shocking or interesting event from *The Twits*. Plan your report on this page.

Date	Newspaper name

Catchy headline

Lead paragraph: Who? What? Where? When?	Picture
	Caption
Details explaining why and how (mostly facts)	Extra information (opinions or quotes from witnesses)

▼ ASSESSMENT

1. Making sense of it

To read aloud and understand the meaning of new words.

Media resource 'Read with expression', interactive activity 'Dahl's dictionary'.

What to do

- Open the media resource 'Read with expression' and read the passage to the class with lots of expression. Ask: *Did you enjoy listening to it? Why?* (The way it is read, using lots of expression, makes it entertaining.) Discuss how expression helps comprehension.

- Read the passage again and ask the children to identify the made-up words ('frumpet', 'grunion', 'swazzle', 'swizzle', 'gnozzle', 'gnosh', 'gnazzle'). Ask: *Do these words make the text difficult to read or understand? Why?* (No, when read with expression, the words can be interpreted in context.)

- Explain the importance of being able to make sense of an unknown word when reading difficult or unfamiliar words: break up the word into syllables or find the root word (for example, 'frump – et'). Spelling rules can help with pronunciation – 'gn' has a silent 'g' ('gnaw', 'gnat', 'sign').

- Ask the children to work in pairs or small groups to explain the words' meaning in context using the interactive activity and share answers with the class.

- Each child should choose a chapter and practise reading it aloud with expression. Assess their reading using a scale of 0–5 to rate expression, fluency, audibility and understanding.

Support: Give children a familiar text to read. Ask them to read the text aloud with expression, then explain the meaning of the words.

Extension: Provide children with an unfamiliar text to read with difficult words. They should read for meaning.

2. Dig deeper

To read independently and understand what they read.

Copies of *The Twits*, printable page 'Reading comprehension', dictionaries.

What to do

- Tell the children that they are going to answer some questions about one particular chapter of the book. Say the words *Fee Fi Fo Fum* in a loud, sinister voice to the class, and ask what comes to mind. Ask: *What connection does this have with the Twits?* (Words spoken by the giant in Jack and Beanstalk, when he smells the boy and wants to eat him. It reminds us of where Mr Twit says he will eat the boys in the tree.)

- Ask the children to read the chapter 'Four Sticky Little Boys' on their own and then answer the questions on printable page 'Reading comprehension'. Limit their time in order to assess who needs extra support. Remind the children to:
  - Understand the context of the text – skim for clues such as chapter title, pictures, first and last sentences.
  - Read the text, identify unfamiliar words and understand them in context. Use a dictionary.
  - Read the questions once to get an idea of what to look out for.
  - Read the text again with the questions in mind.
  - Answer the questions with appropriate detail. It may be helpful to allocate marks for each question in order to indicate how much detail children should provide.

- The questions address different levels of comprehension, such as word level, literal, requiring interpretation and inferences, asking their opinion about something.

Support: Highlight specific literal questions for the children to answer first. Provide extra time at your discretion.

3. Report it

Objective

To speak audibly and fluently with an increasing command of standard English.

What you need

Media resource 'Monkey in a cage', printable pages 'Five animal freedoms' and 'Animal welfare report'.

Cross-curricular link

Citizenship

What to do

- Open the media resource 'Monkey in a cage' and talk about the image shown. Ask: *Is it right or wrong to do this?* Encourage reasons for how the children feel about it – if they feel it is 'OK' or 'cruel', they should say why.

- Show the children an enlarged copy of printable page 'Five animal freedoms'. Ask: *Can animals be happy in a cage?* (Yes, if it is big enough and their needs are met.) *Does Mr Twit comply with this?*

- Tell the children to imagine they are an animal welfare inspector. Provide each child with printable page 'Animal welfare report' to make notes on how the Twits treat animals and to plan an oral report. The oral report should have the following structure:
  - an introduction (the reason for the report)
  - a body (description of findings and evidence)
  - a conclusion (recommendations on what should be done and what should happen to Mr Twit – for example, go to jail, receive a warning, do community service, pay a fine, hand the animals over to the RSPCA, or a combination of these types of punishment).

- Once they have finished planning their reports, ask the children to present them to the rest of the class.

Differentiation

Support: Encourage children to practise their presentations until they feel confident to speak in front of others.

Extension: Invite more confident children to use visual aids or do a multimedia presentation.

4. Monkey Line

Objective

To use punctuation to indicate direct speech; to draw inferences.

What you need

Media resource 'Monkey Line advertisement', printable pages 'Introducing inverted commas' and 'Five animal freedoms'.

What to do

- Open the media resource 'Monkey Line advertisement' and play the audio clip. Ask: *What is being advertised?* (A helpline for monkeys.) *Is it funny or serious?* (Funny.) *What is real and what is fantasy?* (A helpline is real but having one for monkeys is fantasy.)

- Discuss reasons why the monkeys might need to use the Monkey Line – perhaps Muggle-Wump's wife wants to talk about how she feels about living in a cage with her family, or Muggle-Wump wants to discuss how guilty he feels after what happened to the Twits. If necessary, refer the children to printable page 'Five animal freedoms' for further ideas.

- Ask pairs of children to role-play the conversations these monkeys might have with the phone counsellor.

- As an independent task, ask them to plan a conversation in speech bubbles using printable page 'Introducing inverted commas'. They should write the dialogue as if it were part of the story.

- Assess how the children use inverted commas to indicate direct speech, inserting a comma after the reporting clause (for example: The counsellor replied, 'How does that make you feel?') and starting a new line per speaker.

Differentiation

Support: Ask children to go through a chapter in the book, identify direct speech and copy the dialogue to practise this skill.

Extension: Encourage children to use a thesaurus to find alternative words for 'said' and 'replied'.

5. Dear diary...

Objective

To use first-person pronouns in first-person narrative; proofread and edit.

What you need

Copies of *The Twits*, printable page 'Dear diary…'.

What to do

- Display part of the story text on the board. For example: 'As soon as Mrs Twit sat down, Mr Twit pointed at her and shouted, "There you are!"' Ask: *Who is telling the story?* (The narrator.) *What clues are in the text?* (Nouns and pronouns.) *Identify the second and third person pronouns.* (her, you.)

- Now ask the children to imagine they are Mrs Twit. Change the text to be in the first person using the pronouns 'I' and 'me'. ('As soon as I sat down, Mr Twit pointed at me and shouted…')

- Remind the children that when telling a story (narrative) from your perspective, you use first-person narrative – using the pronouns 'I', 'me', 'us'.

- Tell the children to choose to be Mr or Mrs Twit and write a diary entry describing the events in one of the chapters. Let them use printable page 'Dear diary…' to write their neat, edited draft. Assess the following:
  - The diary entry should be written in the first person.
  - That it describes what happened to them (past tense), how they feel and what they think will happen – such as, *Tomorrow I'll get him back!*
  - Their ability to edit their own work and improve accuracy in spelling and punctuation.

Differentiation

Support: Give the children sentences from the story to adapt to first-person narrative. Assist them with the editing process.

Extension: Working in groups of four, invite children to choose a different character (Mr Twit, Mrs Twit, Muggle-Wump, Roly-Poly Bird) and write a diary entry on the same event from their character's perspective.

6. Final review

Objective

To identify themes and conventions in texts.

What you need

A small display of books of various genres, photocopiable page 47 'Book review', interactive activity 'Themes described', poster paper.

What to do

- Refer to the display of books of different genres. Hold up one book at a time. Read the title and blurb and ask the children to identify the type of book and its genre, such as fiction – adventure, or non-fiction – reference book.

- Ask which books the children enjoy, prefer, find interesting or boring and to give their reasons.

- On the board, display the four main writing styles: narrative, expository, descriptive and argumentative. Explain each one. Ask: *Which style did Roald Dahl mostly choose?* (Narrative.) An author's style can additionally be serious, humorous, bizarre, sensitive, informative, poetic, and so on.

- Explain that most stories deal with themes (main themes and sub-themes), or topics and issues. In pairs, ask the children to talk about and note down *The Twit's* themes and report back to the class. Discuss ideas. Link the themes to common expressions or idioms.

- As an independent task, ask the children to complete the interactive activity 'Themes described'.

- Provide each child with photocopiable page 47 'Book review', which they should attempt to complete on their own. Assess their ability to do so.

- When they have completed this task, display the reviews for the children to read and compare – one review may differ from another.

Differentiation

Support: Start a genre search for display in the class. As the children come across a new genre, they can add it to poster paper with examples.

Extension: Challenge the children to design their own review sheet for another book.

Book review

● Answer these questions about *The Twits*.

1. Circle the genres this novel fits into.

> adventure   classics   science fiction   comedy
>   fantasy   historic

2. The author's style appeals to both young and old readers. Describe his style.

_____

3. Choose three themes and explain how they feature in the novel.

> friendship   revenge   team work   respect   values   punishment

   a. _____

   b. _____

   c. _____

4. Choose three characters from the story. Use four adjectives to describe each one.

_____

_____

_____

5. If you were the Roly-Poly Bird, what advice would you give any children wanting to play in the Twits' garden?

_____

_____

_____

SCHOLASTIC

Available in this series:

9781407142203

9781407142197

9781407142241

9781407142227

9781407142234

9781407158754 JAN 2016

9781407142258 JAN 2016

9781407158778 JAN 2016

9781407142289 JAN 2016

9781407142319 JAN 2016

9781407142265 MAY 2016

9781407142272 MAY 2016

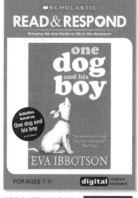

9781407142302 MAY 2016

9781407158761 MAY 2016

9781407158792 MAY 2016

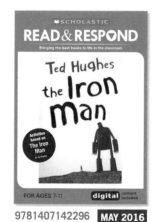

9781407142296 MAY 2016

To find out more, call: 0845 6039091
or visit our website www.scholastic.co.uk/readandrespond